ADVISOR PREP®

CASPER SIM™

FOR THE MIND

2017-2018 EDITION

KEVYN TO M.D

Printed in the United States of America

Second Edition, 2017 e.2

ISBN-13: 978-1944245344

APE Advisor Prep
20 Trafalgar Square
Suite 464
Nashua, NH 03063
Toll Free: 1-844-999-PREP (7737)

Visit us online at:

apetest.com/edu or
caspersim.com

Dedications

"... to all aspiring applicants. May ***God*** Bless you in your endeavors."

Acknowledgments

“Thank you to all of our students for their invaluable input and support”

Disclaimer

This book is presented solely for educational purposes. The publisher is not offering it as legal, or professional services advice. While best efforts have been used in preparing this book, the publisher makes no representations or warranties of any kind and assumes no liabilities of any kind with respect to the accuracy or completeness of the contents. The publisher shall not be held liable or responsible to any person or entity with respect to any loss or incidental or consequential damages caused, or alleged to have been caused, directly or indirectly, by the information contained herein. References when provided are for informational purposes only and do not constitute endorsement of any websites or other sources. Please be aware that the websites listed in this book may change. This book is not intended as a substitute for personalized CASPer® test preparation provided by APE Advisor Prep®.

CASPer® is a registered trademark of Altus Assessments Inc. The CASPer® test is delivered by Altus Assessments at takecasper.com. This website is operated by Advisor Prep Education Services, a provider of test preparation services. Advisor Prep is an independent service provider which has no role in creating or administering the CASPer® test. Altus Assessments and Advisor Prep have no relationship whatsoever, whether by way of affiliation, endorsement, or otherwise.

***conditions apply for rank better and score higher claim.**

Table of Contents

Part 1: CASPer® Fundamentals

Part 2: High-Yield CASPer® Scenarios

Part 3: Sample Model Answers

(this page intentionally left blank)

Welcome to APE

CASPer SIM for the Mind

Are you ready to master CASPer®? Advisor Prep® Education (APE) has been helping applicants just like you excel on CASPer® since the days before the test was a required component of the medical school admissions process in the United States and Canada. A great performance on CASPer® can help you overcome other deficiencies in your application and land you the interview invitation and acceptance you seek.

No one understands CASPer test preparation better than APE Advisor Prep®. We've been successfully mentoring medical school applicants in the United States and Canada seeking admissions into the most competitive Doctor of Medicine (MD) programs for over a decade with stellar results. We excel at getting our students into CASPer® requiring schools and programs.

Before you take the plunge and start preparing for CASPer®, take a step back and ask yourself the following question: Do you see the CASPer® test as an opportunity or a barrier towards your ultimate goal of getting admitted? If you answered the latter, then we encourage you to immediately change your outlook. You should embrace every opportunity to control your performance and the ability to sell your personal and professional characteristics to your desired schools and programs.

How should I use this book?

Congratulations on taking the first and most important step towards obtaining the highest possible rank on the CASPer® test. CASPer SIM™ for the Mind is the original and first book of its kind; a revolutionary guide focusing exclusively on the CASPer® situational judgment test (SJT) first used in the medical school admissions process by the Michael G. DeGroote School of Medicine at McMaster University in 2010.

To get you up and running, we'll walk you through what you need to know (and do) in order to maximize your benefit from this book. **We're going to help you rank better and score higher*.** This book was written to provide background information about the CASPer® test and to act as a companion to compliment APE Director, Inconel™ and Insider students' personalized on-one-one CASPer® test preparation. However, even if you are not an APE Director, Inconel® or Insider student, you'll still benefit from the pearls and tips provided in this book. The expert answers to the most high-yield CASPer® scenarios are designed to act as a springboard to help you brainstorm and arrive towards your own effective answers for the test.

After you have mastered concepts within the first seven chapters of the book, we recommend that you complete the online APE CASPer SIM for the Mind practice tests. These full length practice tests were designed exclusively for this book and contain the same scenarios, taken under simulated test conditions. If you purchased your book directly from APE, you'll find your redemption code located at the back of your book. If your book was purchased from another retailer, you will have to pay a fee to access these online tests. Ensure that you work through and come up with your own answers to each of the scenarios, prior to examining the model answers provided. Please be sure to respect the 5 minute time limit for each scenario to maximize your learning.

To get the most out of this book, we've included the following checklist:

- ☐ **Set a rank score goal** based on the weight given to CASPer® at the schools you're applying to.
- ☐ **Ensure your typing speed** meets the minimum suggested words per minute.
- ☐ **Take the two online Full Length APE Advisor Prep CASPer SIM™ for the Mind tests** under simulated test conditions at https://apetest.com/edu/casper-sim-offer/
- ☐ **Create your study plan** for the CASPer® test based on your performance on APE CASPer SIM™ full length practice CASPer® tests. APE Director, Inconel™ and Insider students, please review your CASPer SIM™ score reports with your mentors.
- ☐ **Review the High-Yield sample answers** provided in this book and meet with your APE mentor on a weekly basis during your CASPer® study preparation.
- ☐ **Practice, practice, practice your time management and content** with the scenarios provided in this book and additional full length practice CASPer® tests available online through APE Advisor Prep® at caspersim.com.

This book is designed to provide basic guidance for the CASPer® test. *It should not be used as a comprehensive study guide for the CASPer® test.* The design of the book is such that the rationales and rubrics behind the specific model answers have been omitted. These answer rationales are discussed during one-on-one review sessions for APE students.

Part 1

CASPer® Fundamentals

Ch01: Introduction to CASPer®

The CASPer® (**C**omputer-based **A**ssessment for **S**ampling **Per**sonal Characteristics) test is a 90 minute online situation judgment test created by McMaster University in Ontario, Canada and administered commercially numerous times per year by Altus Assessments. The computer based test is taken in a non-proctored environment, raising criticism about its validity.

The CASPer® test was previously known as CMSENS (Computer Based Multiple Sample Evaluation of Non-cognitive Skills)

The evaluation of non-cognitive skills (personal and professional qualities) is a crucial component of any medical school admissions process, and has traditionally been assessed through the submission of personal essays, autobiographical submissions, and interviews. The test was originally established as a screening tool to assess prospective medical school candidates' non-cognitive skills prior to the interview. Applicants are ***not tested on any explicit subject knowledge*** and spelling/grammar mistakes are not factored into their results.

CASPer® has been used continuously in the admissions process at the Michael G. DeGroote School of Medicine at McMaster University since 2010 and currently accounts for 32% of an applicant's pre-interview score. It is now a required test at medical schools, residency and allied health programs in the United States, Canada and around the world.

Ch02: CASPer® & the MMInterview

As we previously eluded to, medical schools and affiliated health professional programs evaluate personal and professional qualities in their applicants. Traditionally, this has presented challenges because the current admission models were unable to assess these characteristics with predictive reliability.

The CASPer® test uses open ended questions to capture a broader range of answers from examinees.

In addition to academic achievement, medical schools, nursing schools, dental schools, residency and additional allied health programs value applicants with strong interpersonal skills, integrity and professionalism. This lead to the creation of the Multiple Mini Interview (MMInterview) which is currently the preferred interview format used to screen candidates at many programs in Canada, the United States and around the world.

The MMInterviews were adapted from the objective structured clinical examination (OSCE) to try and minimize interview bias. MMInterviews range from 6-10 minutes per station in length and from 6-18 stations per interview circuit. Compared with traditional interviews, testing an array of domains of competency around personal and professional characteristics, each with a different interviewer, avoids bias attributable to context specificity.

The CASPer® test is essentially an online 90min MMInterview consisting of twelve 5 minute stations.

Fast forward several years and the same team at McMaster University have applied the concept of the MMInterview towards a pre-interview assessment tool. ***CASPer® is essentially an online MMInterview test.***

Similar to the MMInterview, applicants are left in the dark about their CASPer® test performance and often mislead into believing that preparation and practice is not required nor beneficial.

At each section of the test, applicants are allowed five minutes to respond to three follow up questions, after watching a short 1-2 minute video or reading a short descriptive prompt. The average person has a typing speed of 41 words per minute (wpm) with men generally being faster typists than women. This translates to approximately 205 wpm typed on average per scenario on the test.

Being able to type more than 41 wpm does not ensure a high rank on your CASPer® test but having an average typing speed of less than 41 wpm almost guarantees that you **will rank among the bottom third** of all examinees.

The model APE CASPer SIM™ answers provided are based on an average 46 wpm typing speed.

Proper time management is also essential for both the CASPer® test and the MMInterview. You'll want to allow yourself 30 seconds to reread your answers to ensure proper sentence structure prior to submitting your responses because there's no going back once you move on to the next section.

Ch03: CASPer® Format & Scoring

For the 2017-2018 year, the CASPer® test consists of 12 sections (8 videos, 4 non-video). Each section will contain either a short 1-2 minute video (video-based), or a short prompt (word-based), followed by three open-ended probing questions. The examinee will have a total of five minutes to answer all three questions. There is an optional 15 minute break halfway.

As an applicant you'll never see your actual CASPer® test score but it's still important to be familiar with how the test is graded. Unlike other standardized tests with established pass/fail cutoffs, CASPer® is not a pass/fail test but rather a standardized tool for ranking a large number of applicants based on personal characteristics.

Did you know that anyone without a conflict of interest can sign up to be a CASPer® test rater.

Given the short 5 minute time interval for each section, spelling mistakes and grammatical errors are not explicitly factored into an applicant's score. **However, significant spelling mistakes and grammatical errors may take away from the legibility of an answer and based on our experience, may indirectly result in a lower score.**

If there are fewer than 3 weeks before your actual test, don't panic. Be sure to familiarize yourself with the logistics of the test and tested domains presented in the next chapter.

Each section of the test is scored by a different rater using a Likert type scale ranging from 1-9. This means that each completed CASPer® test is ultimately scored by 12 different raters. The raters do not have access to any personal information (such as your name, gender, race, age, etc.). However, the fact that each section of the test is hand scored by a unique rater does make the test more susceptible to rater bias than other computer assessed standardized tests.

While each CASPer® rater is provided with the necessary background and theory for each section, the ***fact that the test is hand scored means that there is an element of subjectivity in how your answers are assessed***. We will exploit this in more detail in subsequent chapters and in the high-yield sample answers provided.

Your final test score is collated from your individual scores, resulting in a maximum total score of 108. Keep in mind that while CASPer® is not designed to be a pass/fail test, the overall outcome is one and the same. Based on our experience, if your total CASPer® score ranks you below the 50th percentile, then your chances of being admitted into any program decrease significantly.

To minimize the effect of rater bias on your score, avoid volunteering your opinion on controversial topics. Focus your answers around your personal experiences instead.

Ch04: Characteristics Assessed

Traditionally, a lack of professionalism accounts for over 90% of all complaints in the medical profession. As a screening tool, CASPer® aims to reduce this number by helping institutions assess personal and professional characteristics deemed important in the practice of medicine, nursing and beyond.

Avoid using point form answers. Stick to full paragraph form answers for CASPer®.

Broadly speaking, the test aims to gain insight into an applicant's core situational competency framework by exposing them to hypothetical video scenarios and behavioral word based scenarios. The situational competency framework can be likened to an applicant's ability to display specific roles such as ***collaborator, communicator, advocate and professional.*** In addition to these important roles, the personal characteristics most commonly assessed on the CASPer® test are: ***Resiliency, Empathy, Self-Reflection, Integrity and Ethical Reasoning.***

Given the relatively subjective nature of CASPer®, simply using buzz words may or may not get you the "score" needed depending on the individual rater. However, buzz words when used appropriately, are helpful at alerting the rater that they should be on the lookout for further evidence demonstrating the mentioned personal characteristic.

When using a buzz word, remember to **back up your buzz word** with personal experience.

Ch05: Is CASPer® Coachable?

Unlike other standardized tests, the creators of the CASPer® test do not provide applicants with explicit learning objectives on how to prepare for the test. ***They hope that applicants will simply take the test "blindly" without any prior preparation***.

Research shows that performance on tests like CASPer are enhanced with prior practice and preparation.

However, we understand that applicants know better. By purchasing this book, you have already taken the necessary step towards excelling on your CASPer® test. With the CASPer® test worth as much as 1/3 of the pre-interview admissions score at select schools, many applicants have been able to benefit from prior preparation for the test.

Broadly speaking, the current literature confirms that individuals can fake their responses on Situational Judgment Tests (SJT) like CASPer®. According to a research study performed by Whetzel and McDaniel (2009), faking on a selection measure refers to deliberate distortion of responses by individuals in order to score favorably. There has been debate as to whether examinees can fake responses on selection measures, and the impact this will have on the test's integrity. Whetzel and McDaniel (2009) stated that the research on faking clearly shows that people can fake responses on SJTs. Faking therefore, can be considered to be one of the documented weaknesses of using SJTs to predict one's performance. Nguyen et al. found that SJTs presented under a behavioral tendency response format like those used by CASPer® could be faked, with effect sizes ranging

When preparing for CASPer®, it is a good idea to create a diary of relevant experiences.

between .15 and .34 (15%-34%).

In terms of coaching and practice effects on SJTs, once again, the current literature supports the conclusion that examinees do benefit from advance test preparation (even for SJTs). One study by Cullen, Sackett and Lievens (2006) examined the coachability of SJTs for consideration as selection instruments in high-stakes testing. Cullen et al. concluded that performance on some SJTs could be enhanced by coaching. In terms of practice effects, Cullen et al. indicated that the retest effects of SJTs are not larger than effects for traditional tests such as cognitive ability tests (ie. MCAT®).

The take home message for applicants required to take SJTs like CASPer® is to be critical and take advantage of resources within their means to optimize their test performance, just as they would for other standardized tests such as the MCAT®. *Be informed and prepared for your CASPer® test.*

References:

Whetzel, D. L., & McDaniel, M. A. (2009). Situational judgment tests: An overview of current research. Human Resource Management Review, 19, 188-202.

Nguyen, N. T., Biderman, M. D., & McDaniel, M. A. (2005). Effects of response instructions on faking a situational judgment test. International Journal of Selection and Assessment, 13, 250-260.

Cullen, M.J., Sackett, P.R., & Lievens, F. (2006). Threats to the operational use of situational judgment tests in the college admission process. International Journal of Selection and Assessment, 14, 142-55.

Ebo K. A Osam (2014) The Adaptation of a Situational Judgment Test to Measure Leadership Knowledge in the Workplace, Western Kentucky University

Ch06: Schools Using CASPer®

As of 2017, the following schools and programs worldwide have adopted CASPer® or are in the process of adopting the CASPer®.

2017-2018

School	Country
Tulane University	USA
New York Medical College	USA
East Tennessee State University	USA
Rutgers University	USA
Central Michigan University	USA
University of Vermont	USA
University of Illinois at Chicago	USA
West Virginia University	USA

McMaster University	Canada
University of Ottawa	Canada
University of Saskatchewan	Canada
Dalhousie University	Canada
University of Waterloo	Canada
University of British Columbia	Canada
McGill University	Canada
University of Alberta	Canada
Universite de Montreal	Canada
College of the Rockies	Canada
Nipissing University	Canada
Conestoga College	Canada
Laval University	Canada

Trent University	Canada
Mohawk College	Canada
North Island College	Canada
St. Francis Xavier University	Canada
York University, School of Nursing	Canada
Deakin University	Australia
Monash University	Australia
Victoria University	Australia
Edith Cowan University	Australia
La Trobe University	Australia
Massey University	New Zealand

To register for the CASPer® test, visit http://takecasper.com and pay your registration fee which consists of a test fee and distribution fee. For 2016-2017, US applicants will be required to pay $20 ($10 test fee + $10 distribution fee) while Canadian applicants will be required to pay $50 ($40 test fee + $10 distribution fees) including applicants applying only to McMaster University, Michael G. DeGroote School of Medicine.

Each CASPer® test is country and discipline specific. You'll have to take CASPer® twice if applying to medical school in the US and Canadian programs.

Ch07: CASPer® Pearls

The following CASPer® pearls are fundamental to achieving success on your CASPer® test. Prior to moving on to the high yield scenarios of this book, please ensure that you have met each objective listed in this chapter.

Improve effectiveness by keeping answers concise for the CASPer® test.

Pearl 1: Ensure you can type a minimum of 45 words per minute (wpm) with minimal errors.

Objective:

Maintain a typing speed of at least 45 wpm for 90 minutes.

If you're a slow typist, you are already at a significant disadvantage compared to other examinees for this test. With only 5 minutes allotted per section, the clock will work against all slow typists. **Typing slowly is a sure recipe for disaster on CASPer®.**

Use buzz words to help focus the rater's attention on your personal experience.

Start by determining your typing speed. There are plenty of typing tutorial sites online that will provide you with this information for free. If your typing speed currently falls below 45 wpm, you'll need to devote extra time and practice in order to bring up your typing speed to the desired level. Do not attempt to fill in the answers to any of the sample CASPer® sections in this book until you're able to confidently and consistently type a minimum of 45 words per minute for a duration of 90 minutes.

Pearl 2: Organize and prioritize your personal experiences on paper.

Objective:

Maintain a diary of your pertinent personal experiences highlighting relevant characteristics assessed.

CASPer® is an open book test administered in a *non-proctored* environment. The creators of this test frequently try and catch examinees off guard by asking about "extreme" events that have occurred in their lives. Anticipate "extremism" and save yourself the panic on test day.

We will use an example involving conflict and failure to get you started. Begin by brainstorming ideas in your mind around conflicts you've experienced and failures you've encountered in life. *Think about what happened, who it involved, what you've learned and what you'd do differently* if faced with the same situation in the future. Now jot down all your thoughts and organize them in a way that will make them easily accessible for you to refer back to on your actual test day. As you write down your experiences, think about relevant buzz words that resonate to the applicable experience you are sharing. Using our example for conflict and failure, the appropriate "buzz" words may include, **resiliency, collaboration, communication and self-reflection.** You don't need to hit every single buzz word but when a buzz word is used, it is important to provide evidence of the buzz word in action within your answer.

Let's discuss the hypothetical answer below:

"I experienced a conflict involving my research supervisor. We disagreed over how to allocate resources for my research project. I was ultimately able to solve this conflict through excellent communication and collaboration skills."

So what did you think about our hypothetical answer above? If you felt that this is exactly the kind of answer you should avoid on your test, then please pat yourself on the shoulder. ***The answer includes relevant buzz words but fails to justify and provide evidence showing how the applicant demonstrated excellent communication and collaboration skills.***

Let's try again with another hypothetical answer.

"I experienced a conflict involving my research supervisor. I felt the research grant money should be used to purchase new equipment for our lab instead of hiring additional staff as suggested by my supervisor. I recognize the importance of open communication and highlighted several benefits of having new equipment that my supervisor had not considered and my supervisor did the same with respect to hiring additional staff. Together we were able to collaborate and compromise to benefit research and everyone in our lab."

Notice that in the second answer, we include "buzz" words to draw the evaluator's attention to our answer **AND** provide justification and evidence showing exactly how the buzz word qualities are demonstrated.

Pearl 3: Be comfortable with the four common tested bioethical principles.

Objective:

Maintain a diary of your pertinent personal experiences as they relate to the most commonly tested bioethical principles.

The four fundamental bioethical principles most commonly tested on the CASPer® test are **informed consent, non-maleficence, confidentiality and beneficence.** We will not get into a detailed discussion of these principles in this book so if you need to brush up on what they are and why they are important, two excellent free online resources are the University of Washington, Department of bioethics guide and the Canadian Medical Association Journal, bioethics for clinicians' series.

As you come up with personal examples for each of these commonly tested ethical principles, ask yourself, *how you were able to demonstrate them and in the cases where they weren't demonstrated, be prepared to explain why.*

Suggested Free Ethics Resources

http://www.cmaj.ca/site/misc/bioethics_e.xhtml

https://depts.washington.edu/bioethx/topics/

Pearl 4: Allocate 30 seconds for proofreading your answers before moving on to the next section.

Objective:

Allow yourself 30 seconds to proofread your answer before submitting your response.

Avoid talking abou negative experiences unles specifically asked about them on th CASPer® test.

Proofreading your answers before moving on can mean the difference between ultimately receiving an interview and a rejection over the course of the entire test. It may seem very obvious, but *only a small fraction of test takers actually do it because of the tight time constraints*.

Pearl 5: Practice your time management by simulating the exact same testing conditions.

Objective:

Maintain a steady pace, and allow yourself four and a half minutes to answer all three follow up questions.

If you accidentally typed your answer to all three questions in one box, do not erase and retype them in subsequent boxes. **Instead, include a word or two in the empty boxes, instructing the rate where to look for the answers.**

The 5 minute response time limit for CASPer® will require you to get used to thinking quickly on your feet. You will need to be able to pull from all your practice examples within your diary. The best way to do this is to practice on as many CASPer® test scenarios as possible. We provide more additional full length practice tests to help you with your time management and content development, delivered over a similar testing interface as the real exam. These are available at: **caspersim.com**

Part 2

High-Yield Scenarios

(this page intentionally left blank)

High-Yield Practice Scenarios

How to get the most out of your preparation

The following CASPer® scenarios have been carefully selected to provide you with the most high-yield practice currently available. To get the most out of your preparation from this book, ensure that your responses are completed online, under the same simulated conditions as your actual test prior to reviewing the sample model answers.

To complete your APE CASPer SIM for the Mind full length tests online, please visit:

https://apetest.com/edu/casper-sim-offer/

Select sample model answers to the practice CASPer® scenarios are included. The remaining answers may be discussed during your APE CASPer SIM™ review sessions for APE students.

If you are not an APE student and would like to learn more about how APE Advisor Prep® can help you improve your CASPer® performance with one-on-one CASPer® testing, please visit:

http://caspersim.com

Section 01: Emotions & Decisions

Sometimes in life, we allow our emotions to affect our decisions.

Describe a situation where your emotions affected an important decision in your life.

How do you approach a decision when you are overwhelmed with emotions?

Individuals who readily show emotions provide an opportunity for people to assess their genuineness. Do you agree or disagree?

Section Notes

Section 02: The Easy Way Out

There are times when it is easier to ignore a behavior than to address it.

Describe a situation you experienced involving a behavior requiring correction that was ignored.

How would you approach an individual whose behavior required correction?

Individuals who fail to address inappropriate behaviors as they arise, display a lack of professionalism. Do you agree or disagree?

Section Notes

Section 03: A Personal Sacrifice

Think about a situation where you unexpectedly made a personal sacrifice.

Briefly describe the situation.

What aspect of your personal sacrifice was the ***least*** appealing to you?

Applying to medical school often requires making sacrifices. How would you handle the situation if you were unsuccessful in your medical school application(s)?

Section Notes

Section 04: Friends & Foes

Recall a situation when you were able to get individuals who dislike each other to co-operate together.

Briefly describe the situation and how you accomplished this?

What might you do differently if faced with a similar task in the future?

How did others respond to your ability to bring two individuals who dislike each other together and how did you handle their reaction?

Section Notes

Section 05: Winning the Jackpot

You are the single winner in a multi-million dollar lottery.

Briefly describe your reason(s) for playing the lottery.

What would be your biggest challenge after winning the multi-million dollar lottery jackpot?

What would you do with your lottery winnings?

Section Notes

Section 06: Meaningful Experience

Think about your most meaningful volunteer experience.

Briefly describe your most meaningful volunteer experience.

What did you learn from this volunteer experience that would benefit your future career as a nurse?

How did your weakness(es) negatively impact on this volunteer experience?

Section Notes

Section 07: Favorite Organization

Think about your favorite organization and why it resonates with you.

Describe your favorite organization and why it resonates with you.

If you could implement one change to this organization, what would it be and why?

The most effective way to support an organization is to donate money to its mission. Do you agree or disagree?

Section Notes

Section 08: Managing Priorities

Recall a time when a situation in your professional life made it challenging to manage your priorities.

Briefly describe the situation.

What did you learn from this experience, and would you do anything differently?

How would you handle a situation if you were unable to cope with your priorities?

Section Notes

Section 09: Starting Residency

There are many aspects to starting a medical residency. Think about the aspects that are the *most* appealing and *least* appealing to you.

What aspect of starting residency do you find the ***most*** appealing?

What aspect of starting residency do you find the ***least*** appealing?

How would you cope with the outcome of being unmatched in your residency application(s)?

Section Notes

Section 10: Professionalism

Medical Students are expected to maintain a high level of professionalism. Recall a situation in your life when you displayed a lack of professionalism.

Briefly describe a situation in your life when you displayed a lack of professionalism.

What did you learn from this situation and what repercussion(s) did you encounter?

What should the penalty be for a student who hands in a plagiarized assignment and gets caught?

Section Notes

Section 11: School of Life

Sometimes, what we experience in life is very different from what we are taught.

Describe a situation where your experience in life differed greatly from what you were taught.

What did you learn from this situation?

How do you approach a task when you do not have enough information?

Section Notes

Section 12: Conflict & Relationships

Conflict and emotions are important components of our relationships. Over time, we become more efficient at managing our emotions and conflict.

Briefly describe a conflict where your emotions affected an important decision in your life.

What advice would you offer a friend who was going through a similar conflict?

How would you cope with a situation involving lateral violence between you and a colleague?

Section Notes

Section 13: Working in a Group

There are many aspects to group work. Think about the aspects that are the most appealing and least appealing to you.

What aspect of group work do you find the ***most*** appealing?

What aspect of group work do you find the ***least*** appealing?

If a member of your group was not participating, how would you handle the situation?

Section Notes

Section 14: A Religious Dilemma

You are an executive producer.
(video url: http://apetest.com/caspersim/section14)

Do you agree with the other two producers' suggestion to terminate Annie's character on the show? Why or why not?

Assume you decide to terminate Annie's character on the show, how would you break this news to her?

Under what circumstances might it be acceptable to give in to peer pressure?

Section Notes

Section 15: Delivering Bad News

Delivering bad news is an inevitable part of being a physician. Recall a time in your life when you had to deliver bad news.

Describe a situation in your life when you had to deliver bad news.

What did you learn from this experience and would you do anything differently?

When might it be appropriate to withhold bad news?

Section Notes

Section 16: A Balancing Act

Think about a situation in your life that required balancing the needs of multiple individuals at the same time.

Briefly describe the situation.

How would you approach an individual that was consistently unable to balance the competing needs of multiple individuals at the same time?

What are some important barriers to being able to balance the competing needs of multiple individuals?

Section Notes

Section 17: From Start to Finish

Recall an important event in your life that you managed from start to finish.

Describe an important event in your life that you managed from start to finish.

What did you learn from this situation and would you do anything differently?

An individual's personal strength can also act simultaneously as a personal weakness. Do you agree or disagree?

Section Notes

Section 18: A Difference of Opinion

Recall a time when your opinion differed from that of your supervisor (or superior).

Briefly describe the situation.

What did you learn from this experience?

Individuals who advocate for themselves are more likely to advocate for others. Do you agree or disagree?

Section Notes

Section 19: Personal Weakness

Reflect on a situation where you displayed a personal weakness.

Briefly describe the situation.

What did you learn from this situation?

How did others react to your weakness and how did you handle their reaction?

Section Notes

Section 20: Doctors as Role Models

Doctors are regarded as role models. Think about a situation in your life where you were regarded as a role model.

Briefly describe a situation in your life where you were regarded as a role model.

Briefly describe the greatest challenge you faced as a role model.

Who do you consider to be a role model and why?

Section Notes

Section 21: Unable to Follow

Recall a situation when you were unable to follow directions or instructions.

Briefly describe the situation and why you were unable to follow directions/instructions.

How would you approach an individual who is unable to follow directions or instructions repeatedly?

Individuals that generally do not follow directions are more likely to make mistakes. Do you agree or disagree with this statement?

Section Notes

Section 22: See One, Teach One

Reflect on a situation in your life where you were an educator.

Briefly describe a situation where you were an educator.

As an educator, how do you know when you have learned enough?

What challenge(s) did you encounter as an educator and how did you overcome them?

Section Notes

Section 23: Access to Medications

Access to free prescription medications is a human right.

Do you agree or disagree with the above statement?

Assume you are a physician and your patient is unable to afford the medication you prescribe, how would you handle this situation?

If you could make one change to the current health care system, what would it be and why?

Section Notes

Section 24: Feeling Overwhelmed

Reflect on the most overwhelming situation you have ever encountered in your life.

Briefly describe the most overwhelming situation you have ever encountered.

What did you learn from this overwhelming situation?

What strategies do you use to help you cope when you are feeling overwhelmed?

Section Notes

Section 25: Expect the Unexpected

Sometimes in life, we must face the unexpected.

Describe a situation in your life where you had to face the unexpected.

How did others respond to your actions and how did you handle their response?

Individuals who struggle with change are more likely to struggle with facing the unexpected. Do you agree or disagree?

Section Notes

Section 26: Mistake in the Kitchen

You are a co-worker in the restaurant.

(video url: http://caspersim.apetest.com/s3/section26)

Should the chef notify the customer that their order was incorrectly prepared?

Assume, the chef decides NOT to notify the customer. How would you handle the situation?

Would you notify the chef's "boss" about the mistake? Why or why not?

Section Notes

Part 3

Sample Model Answers

Answer 01: Emotions & Decisions

Sometimes in life, we allow our emotions to affect our decisions.

Describe a situation where your emotions affected an important decision in your life.

Growing up, I always dreamed about the day when I would buy my first home. When the day finally came, I was torn between an old Victorian house and a new construction. During the home inspection, I learned that there were numerous structural issues with the Victorian house. Since I was in love with the charm of the Victorian house, I decided to ignore this negative information to satisfy my emotions.

How do you approach a decision when you are overwhelmed with emotions?

In hindsight, allowing my emotions to affect such an important decision resulted in a very costly lesson. I've learned to take a step back and separate myself from the situation that is flooding my brain with emotions. I then self-reflect on my options and identify possible solutions. In order to achieve a suitable outcome, I've learned that it's ok to ask for help and to take advantage of my resources, family and support network for advice and wisdom.

Individuals who readily show emotions provide an opportunity for people to assess their genuineness. Do you agree or disagree?

An individual's ability to readily show emotions does not necessarily correlate with an opportunity to assess their level of genuineness. I disagree with this statement because as human beings, our emotions are fluid in nature and can be portrayed in opposite directions from our true intent or level of authenticity. A person's genuineness may be more thoroughly assessed by reflecting on their actions and personal traits.

Notes

Answer 02: The Easy Way Out

There are times when it is easier to ignore a behavior than to address it.

Describe a situation you experienced involving a behavior requiring correction that was ignored.

As a student, my clinical research project required me to analyze patient data. On one occasion, we had several patients experience significant toxicity from the experimental drug we were investigating. My supervisor suggested we fudge the data in order to positively affect the results of our study. This put me in a very difficult position especially since this behavior originated from my superior. I ultimately did not turn a blind eye to their behavior.

How would you approach an individual whose behavior required correction?

In my experience, there are times when it would have been easier to turn a blind eye to certain behaviors. This has not been my philosophy. In these situations, I first identify what the issues are around the behavior. Without jumping to any conclusions, I would listen to the other individual's side of their story. I would then communicate my concerns respectfully and professionally in order to arrive at a mutual outcome for the behavior requiring correction.

Individuals who fail to address inappropriate behaviors after they arise, display a lack of professionalism. Do you agree or disagree?

I agree with this statement. "Doing Right" is a lot easier said than done at times. However, being professional requires an individual to act and respond appropriately to situations in order to maintain the highest standards for their character and discipline. If inappropriate behaviors are being swept under the rug, this results in a lose-lose situation for the individual's ethical responsibilities and their professionalism.

Notes

Answer 03: A Personal Sacrifice

Think about a situation where you unexpectedly made a personal sacrifice.

Briefly describe the situation.

The day I was set to leave New York to attend my best friend's wedding, I received an unexpected call to come into work urgently. I learned that our database system had been hacked. As the lead security specialist for the company, I decided to postpone my flight by 24 hours to stay behind and help patch a security breach and support my fellow team members at this crucial time. In the end, I was still able to attend the wedding and close the loophole.

What aspect of your personal sacrifice was the ***least*** appealing to you?

The possibility of missing my best friend's wedding was the least appealing to me. This is a once in a life time opportunity. However, in my situation, the unexpected compromise of our customers' sensitive information and my company's reputation required that I place my personal needs aside temporarily and advocate for the greater need of everyone else involved. I'm an individual that works well under pressure and I'm very glad everything worked out!

Applying to medical school often requires making sacrifices. How would you handle the situation if you were unsuccessful in your medical school application(s)?

If unsuccessful, I would use this situation as a learning opportunity for future growth. Becoming a physician is a privilege that needs to be earned. I would self-reflect on my submitted application and seek opportunities to strengthen my reapplication candidacy. Personal growth is also important during this off cycle. I would continue to do the things I enjoy such as travelling, cooking and take on a few new challenges while reapplying to medical school.

Notes

Answer 04: Friends & Foes

Recall a situation when you were able to get individuals who dislike each other to co-operate together.

Briefly describe the situation and how you accomplished this?

Working for a charity, my co-workers and I were racing against time to meet an important fundraising deadline. Two co-workers did not care for each other and wanted to complete their portions of the campaign individually rather than as a team. When I presented them with evidence that we would finish hours earlier by working together, they decided to put their differences aside. We finished the campaign early and had time to work on other tasks.

What might you do differently if faced with a similar situation in the future?

If faced with individuals who are less willing to cooperate with each other, I would apply a more direct situation-action-result technique to gain a better understand of the reasons behind their "dislike" for each other. I would also want to facilitate a better understanding of their relationship dynamics as well as the qualities they admire about each other. My goal would be to ensure effectiveness at our jobs while maximizing our work environment together.

How did others respond to your ability to bring two individuals who dislike each other together and how did you handle their reaction?

There was initial shock among our office at how quickly we were able to complete the campaign, given how much work was left. After the initial reaction, we all received praise from our supervisor for our ability to work together. I felt very thankful and appreciative for the compliments we received. This situation helped bring these two coworkers closer and definitely paved the way for future team projects together.

Notes

Answer 05: Winning the Jackpot

You are the single winner in a multi-million dollar lottery.

Briefly describe your reason(s) for playing the lottery.

Taking risks is a part of human nature. In the case of playing the lottery, the negative risk of losing my money is overshadowed by the positive good that results from winning the jackpot. My reasons for playing the lottery are the freedom and increased opportunities afforded by winning the jackpot. With these increased opportunities, I would be able to make a larger positive impact on my community than without winning the lottery.

What would be your biggest challenge after winning the multi-million dollar lottery jackpot?

Maintaining my personal and family's safety would be my biggest challenge after winning such a large sum of money. With my new found financial security, I would take all the necessary steps to maintain my confidentiality such as using a trust fund to claim my winnings rather than disclose my personal information. Afterwards, I would seek additional assistance from professionals to strategize and maximize my own safety and of those around me.

What would you do with your lottery winnings?

I would establish a charity and deposit 50% of my winnings into this foundation. I am very passionate about advocating for individuals (and animals) who do not have a voice. I would continue to devote my time and knowledge to improving their lives. With the assistance of my foundation, this would allow me to increase awareness on issues most pertinent to these populations and further network with and support other like-minded organizations.

Notes

Answer 06: Meaningful Experience

Think about your most meaningful volunteer experience.

Briefly describe your most meaningful volunteer experience.

My most meaningful volunteer experience is being a supervisor for the animal enrichment program at our animal humane society. I have been a volunteer here for over 7 years on a weekly basis. Being able to advocate for animals who are often abused, neglected and without a voice is very difficult at times. However, the benefits are enormous and very rewarding when these animals are adopted or look into your eyes to thank you for your love.

What did you learn from this volunteer experience that would benefit your future career as a nurse?

Humans and animals share many similarities. By responding to non-verbal cues in these animals, I help them cope with the intimidating shelter environment. Similarly, there are many populations whose voices are often unheard of and this negatively affects their health. I've learned to be empathetic to their concerns and through my experience with animals, I'm able to transfer this sensitivity and patience towards my patients as their nurse.

How did your weakness(es) negatively impact on this volunteer experience?

Allowing my emotions to interfere with helping the animals is a weakness that I experienced at the start of this volunteer experience. I became emotional at the site of an abused animal and felt a lot of resentment for the individuals capable of inflicting pain and suffering on an animal. After self-reflecting, I channeled my negative emotions into positive actions such as raising awareness for these animals as well as finding them new homes.

Notes

Answer 07: Favorite Organization

Think about your favorite organization and why it resonates with you.

Describe your favorite organization and why it resonates with you.

My favorite organization is a charity I co-founded with the family members of a close friend whom we lost to suicide in 2013. This organization is very close to my heart because in the days leading up to my friend's suicide, it was clear that there were signs of help that were missed. Our organization is dedicated to advancing LGBTQ mental health and to educate the general public in order to facilitate an increased awareness of mental illness and suicide.

If you could implement one change to this organization, what would it be and why?

One change I would implement would be to have the members of our board of directors meet more regularly. We currently meet once every several months and this results in meetings that are often long and can seem fragmented. Having shorter, more frequent meetings would be more effective from a productivity perspective because it would allow us to discuss how to achieve our goals such as planning events more effectively.

The most effective way to support an organization is to donate money to its mission. Do you agree or disagree?

Money can help support an organization in numerous ways but it is not the most effective way to support an organization. I disagree with this statement. The most effective way to support an organization's mission is to become physically involved in the organization such as volunteering. Through direct involvement, individuals are able to exchange ideas, share their passion and ultimately move forward in achieving the organization's goals.

Notes

Answer 08: Managing Priorities

Recall a time when a situation in your professional life made it challenging to manage your priorities.

Briefly describe the situation.

During my first year of going back to school as a premed student, I was also working full time as an accountant to help support my family. As an accountant, my professional priorities were numerous including responsibilities to my clients. On one specific occasion, I found it challenging to balance being available for my clients professionally during the busy tax season and being available to my family.

What did you learn from this experience, and would you do anything differently?

I learned to plan ahead and anticipate challenges before they arise. The following year, I took the initiative to ensure that my accounting clients were aware of the process from a much earlier date. Ensuring that everyone was on the same page from the start made it much easier to manage all my priorities and alleviated the bottleneck effect around the busy tax season. I was also able to manage my academic/personal priorities subsequently.

How would you handle a situation if you were unable to cope with your priorities?

In such a situation, I would first self-reflect on my priorities and assess how they relate to my professional and personal goals. I am a strong believer that coping skills can be taught, so if I was unable to cope with my priorities, I would communicate my challenges with my peers and colleagues. Being able to ask for help and recognize my own limitations has helped me overcome difficult situations by engaging the assistance of my support network.

Notes

Answer 09: Starting Residency

There are many aspects to starting a medical residency. Think about the aspects that are the *most* appealing and *least* appealing to you.

What aspect of starting residency do you find the ***most*** appealing?

The most appealing aspect of beginning residency is the ability to make significant impacts on my community for the first time as a physician. I'm no stranger when it comes to impacting my community, having done so since my early high school years. However, starting residency will mean crossing over the bridge from medical student to physician and with that comes increased responsibilities, challenges, and personal & professional growth.

What aspect of starting residency do you find the ***least*** appealing?

The least appealing aspect of starting residency is the possibility of having to relocate to another city without my spouse and leaving behind our community. As medical students, we are both very fortunate to be part of this community. Not being able to contribute back to our community as residents during the next phase of our journey is a possibility we will accept but I'm optimistic that things will work out in the end.

How would you cope with the outcome of being unmatched in your residency application(s)?

If I were to go unmatched, I would be disappointed but I would use it as a learning opportunity. I'd start by seeking out support from my mentors and my family. I believe that when one door closes, another one opens and so I would focus on how to improve my residency candidacy for the subsequent cycle and reapply. Throughout this process, I would maintain normalcy and continue with my personal hobbies and take care of my personal health.

Notes

Answer 10: Professionalism

Medical Students are expected to maintain a high level of professionalism. Recall a situation in your life when you displayed a lack of professionalism.

Briefly describe a situation in your life when you displayed a lack of professionalism.

During my first year of college, I took a seminar based course that required giving and attending presentations. On one occasion, I was dealing with an urgent illness in my family and was not able to focus on the presentation being given. During the presentation, I received several text messages from my mom and even though we were in the middle of the presentation, I lost focus of the situation and responded to these messages during the presentation.

What did you learn from this situation and what repercussion(s) did you encounter?

After the end of the presentation, our class was given a pop quiz on the presentation. I ended up performing poorly on this quiz because of my earlier distractions. Reflecting on the situation and taking full responsibility for my actions, I realized that the situation should have been handled very differently. In the future, I will respectfully and quietly excuse myself from my environment before attending to urgent matters that require immediate assistance.

What should the penalty be for a student who hands in a plagiarized assignment and gets caught?

This student should receive a failing grade for their assignment with no opportunity to redo the assignment. In addition to a failing grade, they should receive mentorship on how to avoid plagiarism in the future. If this individual is a repeat offender, then I believe they should face additional consequences such as academic dismissal from their program or school. Academic dishonesty negatively affects everyone and should never be tolerated.

Notes

Answer 11: School of Life

Sometimes, what we experience in life is very different from what we are taught.

Describe a situation where your experience in life differed greatly from what you were taught.

I took a pharmacology course in my third year of college. This course was fascinating because I was immersed in drug mechanisms and learning about the therapeutic uses for these medications. After the course was over, I subsequently volunteered at a hospital pharmacy. It became very obvious that what I experienced as a volunteer regarding how the medications were prescribed, differed greatly from what I had learned about in class.

What did you learn from this situation?

I learned that no amount of teaching in school could fully prepare me for my experience in the real world. In the case of pharmacology, the real world experience about the drug indications differed from the theoretical principles I learned. Such differences positively contributed further to my learning because I sought assistance from my peers in the hospital to translate my classroom learning into real world applications.

How do you approach a task when you do not have enough information?

When faced with a task that requires more information, I begin by self-reflecting on my current knowledge as it relates to the task. To do this, I write down my understanding of the task in terms of important concepts and jot down areas of knowledge I lack. I then create a plan and proceed to seek out resources to acquire this knowledge. The most common resources I've sought out in such situations have been my mentors, teachers, family and technology.

Notes

Answer 12: Conflict & Relationships

Conflict and emotions are important components of our relationships. Over time, we become more efficient at managing our emotions and conflict.

Briefly describe a conflict where your emotions affected an important decision in your life.

For over 10 years, I was a victim of bullying. This physical and verbal abuse has invoked many emotions inside of me. At first, like many victims of bullying, I chose to keep my conflict and emotions hidden. However, as I grew older and more mature, I realized that my sense of fear was hindering my ability to resolve my conflict and negatively affecting my health. As a result, I reached out for support and help to put an end to my bullying once and for all.

What advice would you offer a friend who was going through a similar conflict?

I would ensure that I actively listen to my friend's thoughts and concerns. My advice would be to not keep emotions bottled up inside which I know is easier said than done. In the case of bullying, identifying a support network to openly discuss feelings and fears will go a long way in keeping them healthy. I would also suggest that we brainstorm together on what they think is the best solution moving forward to tackle and prevent future episodes of bullying.

How would you cope with a situation involving lateral violence between you and a colleague?

I would begin by self-reflecting on specific incidents where lateral violence has taken place between us. I would review the events in my mind and ask myself if I may have contributed to the situation. I do not believe that individuals should have to "cope" with situations that are harmful to their mental health in the way that lateral violence surely is. I would advocate for policies that educate, treat and prevent lateral violence in all environments.

Notes

Answer 13: Working in a Group

There are many aspects to group work. Think about the aspects that are the most appealing and least appealing to you.

What aspect of group work do you find the ***most*** appealing?

The most appealing aspect of group work is the ability as a team, to take a complex project and break it down into smaller components and steps. One such project I was involved in was a research presentation on diabetes. By collaborating as a group, we were able to receive and give input on concepts and tasks related to our diabetes project. Ultimately, the learning we received as a group was significant to advancing diabetes research.

What aspect of group work do you find the ***least*** appealing?

The amount of time that may be required to coordinate with everyone's schedule. In my psychology class, we had several group projects to complete. While I greatly enjoy group work, I found it initially challenging to agree upon a meeting time that would work for everyone. We each ended up compromising one aspect of our schedules. Afterwards, it was smooth sailing and the experience helped us all become more efficient at prioritizing our lives.

If a member of your group was not participating, how would you handle the situation?

I would not jump to any conclusions regarding the reasons why they are not participating. In this situation, I would want to assess the other group members' level of participation to see if there are any group dynamics that are contributing to this member's lack of input. It's important to respectfully discuss with all members of the group any concerns that may exist. I would also ask this member of the group how they felt the team's group work was progressing.

Notes

Answer 15: Delivering Bad News

Delivering bad news is an inevitable part of being a physician. Recall a time in your life when you had to deliver bad news.

Describe a situation in your life when you had to deliver bad news.

> *As a manager of a seasonal business, we are faced with fluctuations that arise in the economy. During the fall of the housing market, our business was especially affected by the change in consumer spending. Due to the significant budget cuts we experienced, I was faced with the difficult decision of telling several valued team members that they were going to lose their job because we simply could not afford to keep them on.*

What did you learn from this experience and would you do anything differently?

> *I learned that there is always room for improvement no matter how many times you've had to deliver bad news. In my situation, being able to separate the professional aspect from the personal aspect of my relationships allowed me to focus more effectively on the task of delivering bad news. However, in the future, I will work to improve my clarity as I'm delivering bad news as well as my ability to answer questions and provide support afterwards.*

When might it be appropriate to withhold bad news?

> *It is inappropriate to withhold bad news for an extended period of time. However, when an individual is not in a proper private environment for delivering or receiving bad news, one should wait until an appropriate environment can be found. Also, if the bad news may negatively harm a person's safety, such as if they are currently driving or operating dangerous equipment, then this bad news should be withheld until it can be delivered safely.*

Notes

Answer 16: A Balancing Act

Think about a situation in your life that required balancing the needs of multiple individuals at the same time.

Briefly describe the situation.

I was a secretary for three physicians, each of whom had their own thriving practice with their own set of needs and expectations. In order to balance the needs of multiple individuals, I had to ensure I was aware of their priorities and my responsibilities/limitations. This ultimately allowed me to manage the administrative needs of all three physician practices while simultaneously balancing the individual needs of each physician successfully.

How would you approach an individual that was consistently unable to balance the competing needs of multiple individuals at the same time?

I would seek to understand their difficulties in a supportive and approachable manner. If this individual was my colleague, I would approach them as a friend in a private environment. I would actively listen to them and ask them what they think are some possible solutions. Only after hearing their story and understanding any challenges, will I be able to make an informed decision on how to offer them my support and share my experiences as needed.

What are some important barriers to being able to balance the competing needs of multiple individuals?

Understanding the priorities of each individual and how they relate to your priorities is the biggest barrier to balancing competing needs. Another important barrier is acknowledging your own personal limitations. In my example, I was aware of my own limitations and recognized when/how to ask my senior secretarial team members for support in order to efficiently complete tasks and balance the needs of all three physicians.

Notes

Answer 17: From Start to Finish

Recall an important event in your life that you managed from start to finish.

Describe an important event in your life that you managed from start to finish.

As founder of a small charity dedicated to improving mental health, we host an annual silent auction fundraiser. Initially, I was involved with running the entire charity. I single-handedly managed everything that needed to be done related to our silent auction, from communication, raising awareness, selecting the venue to marketing the event. The event raised over $50,000 and drew a few local celebrities and has since grown internationally.

What did you learn from this situation and would you do anything differently?

I learned how to improve my time management. There were times during the planning of the silent auction when I was being pulled in all directions. Reflecting on my experience, this could have been prevented with more effective time management. For subsequent fundraisers, instead of trying to do everything myself, I learned how to accept help from those around me and work collaboratively together to raise money for mental health.

An individual's personal strength can also act simultaneously as a personal weakness. Do you agree or disagree?

I agree with this statement. A personal strength can also simultaneously act as a double edged sword. In some situations, being detail oriented is a huge asset, but in others, it may lead to inefficiency, resulting in missing a deadline. I can definitely relate to this as I'm very detail oriented. There were times where I came close to missing important deadlines because I initially wasn't able to balance my trait both as a strength and weakness.

Notes

Answer 18: A Difference of Opinion

Recall a time when your opinion differed from that of your supervisor (or superior).

Briefly describe the situation.

Working in the fast paced retail environment as an assistant manager, our store experiences a high employee turnover rate. My manager felt that we should completely eliminate our turnover rate at all costs. While I understand the importance of keeping our employee turnover rate low, this should not come at the expense of our customers or business. In this situation, it is important to spend more time examining the reasons behind the turnover rate.

What did you learn from this experience?

When faced with differences, the ability to compromise is paramount towards reaching a common goal. I emphasized to my manager the importance of eliminating our turnover rate by proposing a compromise: the implementation of a new system of exit interviews to better understand why employees leave or are terminated. Since the implementation, we have learned a lot from our employees and have significantly reduced turnover rates.

Individuals who advocate for themselves are more likely to advocate for others. Do you agree or disagree?

I disagree with this statement because it is suggestive that an individual who is able to speak up for themselves is more likely to speak up for others. This is presumptive and the reality of whether an individual is likely to advocate for others is much more complex. It depends on the strength of the relationship among the individuals because as a parent, I know that I would have no hesitation advocating for my children's well-being before mine.

Notes

Answer 19: Personal Weakness

Reflect on a situation where you displayed a personal weakness.

Briefly describe the situation.

> *I place great emphasis on being "there" for all individuals in my life. Unfortunately, this inability to say "no" resulted in a personal weakness of taking on more than I was capable of. A specific example involved committing to be the maid of honor at my sister's wedding and running a 10km marathon with my best friend on the same day! It was clear that even with my best intentions, my actions had backfired and negatively affected my relationships.*

What did you learn from this situation?

> *I learned that in order to support others, you may have to put yourself first in order to stay healthy. In my situation, the excess stress and pressures I placed on myself over many years affected my vital functions such as sleep and mentation. By recognizing the significant toll that this weakness had on me, I was able to self-reflect and take the necessary measures to restore proper balance to my life. Only then was I in a proper position to help others.*

How did others react to your weakness and how did you handle their reaction?

> *I was scared to tell others about my weakness. However, after speaking with them, their immediate response was filled with guilt and support. They were not aware that this personal weakness existed because I had spent so many years concealing it from others. However, in hindsight they could see the negative impact it had on my health. I was very appreciative of their support and asked that they not feel guilty about my past decisions.*

Notes

Answer 20: Doctors as Role Models

Doctors are regarded as role models. Think about a situation in your life where you were regarded as a role model.

Briefly describe a situation in your life where you were regarded as a role model.

> *In my first year of college, I helped create a lesbian, gay, bisexual, transgendered (LGBT) alliance organization at the college. There was a clear need for such an organization to help advocate for LGBT issues. The initial environment at our college was not the most supportive for LGBT individuals and my idea was initially met with resistance. However, 5 years later, the LGBT alliance remains an active an important community at my college.*

Briefly describe the greatest challenge you faced as a role model.

> *Gathering support from our executive college members to gain approval for an LGBT alliance organization was the biggest challenge. To do so, I had to identify and gain support from a senior faculty mentor for our proposed group and successfully answer questions related to the needs for our proposed group from opposing individuals. Our compassion and use of evidence-based medicine helped successfully advocate for this minority group.*

Who do you consider to be a role model and why?

> *A role model is a person that other people look up to in order to help determine appropriate behaviors. As such, role models can be either positive or negative. I consider my mom to be my most positive role model because for as long as I can remember, I have always looked up to her and looked to her for guidance in life. Over the years, she has taught me so much about respect, dignity, love, compassion and she has sacrificed so much to put others first.*

Notes

Answer 21: Unable To Follow

Recall a situation when you were unable to follow directions or instructions.

Briefly describe the situation and why you were unable to follow directions/instructions.

When I started my job as a regional manager of a pharmaceutical company, I was given several projects to complete. I was still integrating into my new environment and actually had a lot of questions about these projects. However, as a newly hired employee, I set up my own roadblock by thinking that it would be received as a sign of weakness to acknowledge that I didn't grasp the project goals and required clarification of the directives.

How would you approach an individual who is unable to follow directions or instructions repeatedly?

I would treat them as though they were my own family and not make any assumptions about why directions are not being followed. It's important to allow them to explain how they think things are going with respect to their task and if there are any perceived difficulties. Afterwards, as a team member, I would ask them specific questions about the instructions and offer my support by asking them if we could work together on their task/project.

Individuals that generally do not follow directions are more likely to make mistakes. Do you agree or disagree with this statement?

I agree with this statement because directions/instructions often contain detailed information to assist us on how something should be completed, operated, or assembled. When we skip the instructions, we may place our own safety and those around us in danger. A few months ago, I rushed to put together a dining chair without reading the instructions. I ended up ruining my chair and making a mistake because several of the parts were very similar!

Notes

Answer 22: See One, Teach One

Reflect on a situation in your life where you were an educator.

Briefly describe a situation where you were an educator.

I was a computer science teaching assistant (TA) for 2 years at my university. As a TA, I was involved in grading, exam proctoring and student mentoring. I often took difficult concepts and presented them in an easy to understand manner. On one occasion, a student in our course was struggling and on the brink of failure 6 weeks into the course. After making a study plan with tutoring, they were able to successfully complete the course with no further issues.

As an educator, how do you know when you have learned enough?

As a TA, one parameter I use to help me establish when I've learned "enough" is to assess my ability to successfully teach course material to someone with no prior knowledge of the subject. If I can simultaneously engage in a thought provoking discussion about relevant future issues in the same subject at an advanced level with an expert in the subject, then this affords me to opportunity to move on and learn additional, advanced materials.

What challenge(s) did you encounter as an educator and how did you overcome them?

Teaching students with a wide variety of learning styles is a challenge I've encountered. As a TA, I often made written summaries for my students. However, I found that a few of them struggled to understand the material. I sought direct feedback from these students. It became clear that they were visual learners. I've overcome this challenge by taking into account the different learning styles in my lessons in subsequent semesters as a TA.

Notes

Answer 23: Access to Medications

Access to free prescription medications is a human right.

Do you agree or disagree with the above statement?

I disagree that free prescription coverage access is a fundamental human right. A large majority of our health ailments requiring prescription medications are the direct consequences of the choices we make in life. We have a responsibility to the choices we make as they affect our health. In reality, our health care system has finite resource allocations and therefore, access to prescription medications is an individual's responsibility and not a human right.

Assume you are a physician and your patient is unable to afford the medication you prescribe, how would you handle this situation?

As a physician, I would advocate for my patient and explore avenues to maximize their health. If they are not able to afford prescribed medication, I would examine cheaper alternatives such as "generics". However, if this was not an option, I would communicate with drug manufacturers and/or state/provincial government bodies to seek their support in helping offset my patient's costs associated with their medication.

If you could make one change to the current health care system, what would it be and why?

A significant number of preventable hospital errors occur every year resulting in hundreds of thousands of patient deaths worldwide. One change I would make is to improve transparency for patients and their families. If patients were empowered with as much information about health care and education as they are about general consumer products, there would be a dramatic improvement in the quality of our current health care system.

Notes

Answer 24: Feeling Overwhelmed

Reflect on the most overwhelming situation you have ever encountered in your life.

Briefly describe the most overwhelming situation you have ever encountered.

My best friend committed suicide three years ago. In the month leading up to his death, he had issued numerous verbal comments to myself and his family, indicating that the world would be a better place if he wasn't in it and on one occasion, he explicitly stated his intention to commit suicide. However, because of his jovial personality and the fact that I felt that I knew him so well, I did not explore his comments further until it was too late.

What did you learn from this overwhelming situation?

I learned it's very important not to take anyone for granted. In my situation, I had known my friend for many years and this bias unfortunately caused me to react in a different manner than had the same information originated from a stranger. In hindsight, my most overwhelming situation has painfully taught me that when an individual's safety may be compromised, it is important to explore this further, recognize your limitations and ask for support.

What strategies do you use to help you cope when you are feeling overwhelmed?

Finding balance between the different important aspects of my life is the key to coping when I'm feeling overwhelmed. Strategies that have helped me during these times include letting off some steam by confiding with my family and spending more time with them. I also find it very helpful to write down thoughts that come to mind during these experiences. By doing so, I am able to reflect down the road and seek comfort on past situations I've overcome.

Notes

Answer 25: Expect the Unexpected

Sometimes in life, we must face the unexpected.

Describe a situation in your life where you had to face the unexpected.

A few days before my twentieth birthday, my older brother was hit by a car while crossing the street. Unfortunately, he didn't make it. We were extremely close and without any warning, my world came crashing down. Like the average twenty year old, I was immature and unprepared to deal with death. However, I took it upon myself to seek out extra support from my friends and family. I still miss him a lot but recognizing my limitations helps me tremendously.

How did others respond to your actions and how did you handle their response?

I became a recluse, avoided my friends and stopped doing things I had previously enjoyed. My grief and subsequent depression lasted several years and during this dark time, my family and friends never stopped being supportive and there for me. I regret my response, because I neglected those who cared most about me during this difficult time. It has been challenging but I have learned to show compassion to others during difficult moments in life.

Individuals who struggle with change are more likely to struggle with facing the unexpected. Do you agree or disagree?

I agree with this statement. An important aspect to consider is resiliency; an individual's ability to bounce back from hardship. Change often accompanies or must be considered when facing the unexpected. Dealing with unexpected events also scrutinizes an individual's personal resiliency and ability to adapt. As a result, if an individual is more likely to struggle with change, then they may also see the unexpected as change and consequently struggle.

Notes

The following pages are excerpted from the book:

Multiple Mini Interview for the Mind

ISBN: 9781635878400

“During each encounter, you will be expected to complete a task and for most stations, the interviewer will follow up with a standardized set of probing questions to engage you in further discussion. Some programs will provide you with blank paper and a clipboard to write down your thoughts but the vast majority of programs will not. Our suggestion is to work through your interview preparation with the assumption that you will not be able to take notes.

The types of MMInterview stations you’ll encounter on interview day can essentially be grouped into one of the following categories:

1) **Ethical Stations**
2) **Cultural Competency Stations**
3) **Social Issues/Health Policy Stations**
4) **Role Playing Stations**
5) **Collaboration Stations**
6) **Traditional Interview Stations**
7) **Writing Stations**
8) **Video Stations**
9) **Rest Stations**

We’ll explore each category in more detail.

Ethical stations will describe a common scenario whereby a fundamental ethical principle is at risk or has been violated and require you to identify and discuss important issues around that ethical principle as it applies to that scenario. The fundamental ethical principles are beneficence, do no harm, justice, autonomy and consent.”

"Broadly speaking, the current benefits of the MMInterview format can be summarized into direct benefits for the administering program and for individual applicants.

MMInterview - Direct Applicant Benefits

- Greater Number of First Impressions
- Greater Fairness and Transparency
- Greater Faculty Engagement & Exposure
- Greater Number of Independent Encounters

MMInterview - Direct Program Benefits

- Greater Reliability and Validity
- Fewer Interviewer Biases
- Greater Flexibility in screening for desired traits
- Greater Number of Candidates can be screened

"General Approach to Acting & Role Playing Stations

Interviewees frequently cite role playing stations as being one of the most challenging categories because of their artificial settings and the their unpredictable paths. You can't change the settings of these stations but with a few tricks we'll go over, we'll show you how to take control of these scenarios and keep the ball in your court.

Contrary to popular belief, the most important aspect of this role playing scenario is not to deliver the bad news regarding the results of Mr. Reed's prostate biopsy. When faced with a role playing scenario such as this one, it is crucial to first determine the situational context displayed by the actor and to identify background cues. **Rushing in to deliver bad news prematurely often proves to be a very costly mistake in these stations.**

What is bad news?

Quite simply, bad news may be defined as "any information which adversely and seriously affects an individual's view of his or her future" [1]. Delivering bad news is complex and in addition to the verbal component of disclosing bad news, it also includes responding to patients' emotional reactions, involving the patient in decision-making, dealing with the stress created by patients' expectations for cure, the involvement of multiple family members, and the dilemma of how to give hope when the situation is bleak [2].

Why is delivering bad news important?

How bad news is disseminated to patients' will affect….."

CPSIA information can be obtained
at www.ICGtesting.com
Printed in the USA
BVHW04s0731130818
524321BV00013B/397/P

9 781944 245344